# Diamonds in the Rough

## UNCOVER THE WOMAN
## OF BRILLIANCE

## SHANICA L. BELL

Good Fruit Publishing Company
Kenosha, WI 53141

**FOR INFORMATION CONTACT:**
Shanica Bell Ministries
PO Box 883
Kenosha, WI 53141
(888) 773-4764

Please visit our website at
www.shanicabell.com
Online ordering is available for all products.

Printed in the USA by Mira Publishing, St. Louis, MO

*In Loving Memory*

Blossie Mae Clark "Grandma"
November 23, 1919 - October 15, 2010

Evangelist Joyce Ralston "Mommy Joyce"
January 12, 1954 - January 22, 2013

# Dedication

Dedicated to those precious jewels that have inspired and blessed me along the way through their diamond stories; to my mother Nancy Brigham, the most beautiful gemstone I know. I've witnessed your rough places and I've seen God restore your brilliance! He's not finished with you yet. I love you. To my daughter, Shaniya, my most precious gemstone; your story has yet to be told, but with confidence I know that it will be a brilliant one! Always remember your pressure has purpose. I love you!

# Contents

# Foreword

*It is so amazing to me how God processes us like diamonds. Each step is significant and strategic in the revealing of the finished product. First we're hidden from the world, excavated, and then crushed. At those times we are beaten small for the Master's use, but in the fullness of time, it is revealed who we really are created to be. Through authoring, "Diamonds in the Rough", Shanica's revelation of the scriptures unfolds the depths of how God processes each one of us. That scripture is still being written and our willingness to be transparent reveals to us a journey and an excavation to the top!*

Prophetess Wanda L. Bodden
Founder, *Ministry in Motion Global Ministries*
*Port Arthur, TX*

# Introduction

Some say they are a girl's best friend. Many believe they symbolize wealth, fame, and strength. The polished diamond as we know it, glitters and dazzles, and is known as the King of Gems. Something crafted so beautifully must be handmade and custom-designed by a skillfully trained man, with gentle hands and a vision on His mind. He must be a man who knows about natural beauty as well as the importance of inner beauty. He must be equipped with an expensive tool collection to transform the rough stone into the beautiful, brilliant diamond that take so many in with its vast array of beauty and elegance.

The beautiful diamonds that we see on display under lock and key were not always beautiful. They didn't always sparkle or glisten in the lights or captivate onlookers. Their beginning is a humble one – one that begins with a tremendous amount of pressure and travail. The creation of the beautiful gems we see today is a process that begins with a stem of tremendous pressure, but in the end it blossoms a timeless treasure.

I believe that in God's creation of the Heavens and the Earth, he designed a plan so marvelous and intricate for the diamond, especially for us women to see, young and old alike. Yes, we all love diamonds, not just us girls, but men and women alike. If we really look a little deeper into the story behind the stone, we'll notice God's handiwork, wonderfully demonstrated miles below the Earth's surface. I find it fascinating to know that if He cared so much for this piece of molten rock formed miles below the Earth, how much more would He care for us and take us from the pit of pressure to a position of prosperity. Every woman has a diamond experience that will bring out the gem in her – but only if she is processed by the Master Gemologist who only sees the best in her and is the only One capable of bringing it out.

I don't know where you are today. You may be in a rough season or you may already be walking in your brilliance. Wherever you may be, I pray God continues to process you for His purpose to be fulfilled in your life. If you are in a rough place, it is time for those dreams and visions to be birthed out. What you are going through is not meant to break you down, but it was purposed to bring you to a place of brilliance.

# CHAPTER ONE

## Birthing of Precious Stones

*And the rib, which the Lord God had taken from man, made he a woman, and brought her unto the man.* Genesis 2:22

Many associate birth with pain. In fact, if you ask any woman who has given natural birth, I am sure birth and pain will be synonymous. As in any birth we know there will be pain, but we also know there is a purpose that follows the pain if we learn to embrace it. Out of the pain in birthing, a new mother brings forth new life and instantly remembers her pain no more (John 16:21). The Bible tells us that she forgets her travail because of her joy. You may think that the pressure and travail that you are experiencing now will never yield anything beautiful. You may think that you will never get back to that place of joy and happiness because you have found yourself in a rough place. Do you believe that there is a place that you can get to where you can forget your pain and fully embrace your purpose in joy? There is! Each and every one of us was created with a purpose, according to God's plan for our lives (Jeremiah 1:5). Your pressure has purpose and I believe that every woman has her own diamond story, simply because every woman has had her fair share of travail, pressure, and pain. Through her pain, trials, and triumphs she is embedding her own rough story in the testimonial tablet of her heart. Even if she doesn't realize her potential, she has a major role to shine in. She's a mother, a daughter, sister, a friend, or a boss. She's the pastor's wife, or your child's teacher; she may even be the woman next door. She is you.

If you're reading the pages of this book, I am here to tell you that you are a gem. You are a benefit and an asset and never a liability to anyone. No matter what walk of life you have come from, you are still a gem! Our paths may all be different, but we have all been down life's rough roads, experienced seasons of painful turns, and weathered the rage of destiny's storms.

## PURPOSE OF YOUR PRESSURE

What is your purpose you may be wondering? Sometimes we question those rough places that we encounter in life and we wonder why God would allow us to remain there. Do you know that the pressure that you experience is necessary for not only your survival, but for the survival of that dream, vision, book, or business that God has placed down on the inside of you? There is greatness ready to be birthed with purpose right out of your very existence. Did you know that without pressure the beautiful diamonds we see would not exist?

In their humble beginning, the only way for rough diamonds to be created is deep within the Earth's interior under a lot of pressure in extreme conditions. Formation of the rough begins through a squeezing process among carbons, and just enough pressure begins to cause those carbons to crystallize. Isn't that how it is sometimes? It's those high-pressure moments that create you.

Once crystallized, the rough begins to ascend to the surface by attaching itself to rare molten rock originating by violent volcanoes. How amazing! Like a baby in the interior of its mother's womb being brought forth by laboring contractions, there's a diamond out there covered in molten rock ascending through a violent volcano. I often say, for every volcano that erupts, a diamond is born. We often have the mindset that when things erupt in our lives that it's always catastrophic. Eruptions can be devastating, but every eruption in your life doesn't have to yield the worse. Something beautiful can come out of your pain, but only if you can endure the process. Those of us who know God have learned that our pressure soon turns to praise, but only if we stay in Him and go through the process. Only God, the Master Gemologist knows just what to do with something that has been through a tremendous amount of pressure. He knows how to take you through those rough places in your life and process you into the precious jewel that you were created to be. There may just be a prize in the midst of the upheaval of things in your life and just because things appear to be covered in layers of hard days, troublesome times, and worrisome years - if you give it over to God, I promise you, it'll be a beautiful transformation.

Isn't it wonderful how God mindfully created the rough deep within the pit of the Earth's darkness, out of the sight of man, appointing it a set time to surface for the purpose of being one of the world's most prized treasures? What a blessing it is to know that God thought enough about the molten covered rock to use volcanoes as elevators for its elevation and transition into a new dimension. If God can use something as ugly and as catastrophic as a volcano and hard layers of molten rock to be elevators for diamonds, you better know that even the ugly stuff in your life God can use. He can take all those years of hardness and turn it into something brilliant and beautiful.

Had it not been for extreme heat and pressure, the diamond would not have a chance in this world. In fact, the pressure *prepared it* for the next level. The pressure *equipped it* with the necessary elements to make it in the new stage of life. Yes, He certainly has a plan for your very life, too. There is no need to worry or fret over whatever situation that is presenting itself in your life today. God knows just about how much it takes to cause you to ascend out of your rough place to the next level. Instead of hardness, you'll be covered with goodness, if you endure the process.

The Rock of Ages has you covered, and just as the rough is brought out of the volcanic pit, beautified in His glory and later displayed in a locked jewel case, so will God bless you in elevation naturally and spiritually. As God continues to process you for the fullness of His great plan for your life – I want you to know that from this moment on, just like a polished diamond born out of the ashes, you will be able to walk in the fullness of your vast array of beauty, elegance, and brilliance as a woman created in the image of your Creator. Some of your dreams and visions that you're birthing out in those rough places are about to catapult you into your destiny!

# Eve

*And the rib, which the Lord God had taken from man, made he a woman, and brought her unto the man.* Genesis 2:22

# CHAPTER TWO

## You're Wonderfully Made

*I will praise thee; for I am fearfully and wonderfully made:*
*marvelous are thy works; and that my soul knoweth right well.*
Psalms 139:14

She was born out of her husband, mature, complete and ready to be his helpmeet. Just like the rough, he mindfully created Eve from within her husband, from his rib. The word diamond is derived from the Greek word *adamao*, which means *I tame* or *I subdue*. Subdue means to conquer, to tone down and tame as being brought from the wilderness into a domesticated state or under subjection. *Woman of Brilliance –* just like the diamond, you are more than a conqueror and able to tame any situation. You are multifaceted and able to take on multiple projects at one time at work and then come home and cook a full course meal for your family. You also understand the role you have in your position as you subject yourself as a helpmeet.

God didn't choose just any structural member of the body to create you. The rib is defined by the American College Dictionary as *a structural member, which supports the shape of something.* Let's look at it from this perspective, you were created to bring some structure as a help to your husband. Your framework is to support the shape of something. In fact you are the framework of something exquisite! Is it your business you support? Do you support your family, church or husband? Every woman should support something. If nothing else, you should support yourself. Sometimes we get caught up in supporting others that we forget to support ourselves. Support and nurture those dreams that you have. Don't end up wasting precious time and years supporting something or someone unfulfilling and meaningless.

If there is one thing I've learned is that there's nobody like Jesus. And there's nobody who knows me better than my Father who created me. Enjoy being the woman that you were created to be by spending time with your Creator and learning what He has gifted you with. Eve was created with a unique purpose and destiny already embedded in her. She knew her role as a helpmeet the first time she laid her eyes on Adam. Eve supported the man that God brought her out of by helping him tend to the grounds and the Word of God tells us that she was a helpmeet, created for two specific purposes. After God saw that it was not good for man to be alone, he *made* Eve for the purpose of *companionship* and she was *designed* with the responsibility of *helping* her mate. She was created to meet or come in connection to, or satisfy her husband.

Now, this is where some of you women have dropped the ball. Many of you have become a helpmeet to someone that is not your husband and some of you are helping someone who is not able to be met with help. In order for Eve to walk in her divine purpose as a helpmeet for Adam and to ultimately become to Mother of All Living, he had to be *doing something*. He had to be that something she needed to support the shape of. Somebody may have to go back and read that again! Eve could not meet him with help if he were just lying around the Garden of Eden all day. No, Adam's job was to dress and keep the garden. He was a landscaper. God, his boss, gave him those specific instructions. Eve was created to meet Adam with any of his needs as a companion with a responsibility as a married woman, caring about pleasing her husband.

I know many of you are saying, *"I'm not married"*. Well, if you are not married you are still fearfully and wonderfully made. You should have a natural desire to be a helpmeet. But as an unmarried woman we are instructed by the word of God to *care for the things of the Lord that you may be holy in body and in spirit* (I Cor. 7:34). Support the Lord, get in tune with what he desires for you to accomplish while you're unmarried. It doesn't matter what your marital status is, I believe that we are living in a realm where God has something great for all of His daughters, His diamonds, whether we are married or not. Your purpose should be your pursuit, seeking out the one who calls you according to His purpose. God has gifted you with something life changing and something of value. Remember you are designed to be a more than a conqueror, so stay in the fight. You were designed with a one of a kind gift, with a one of a kind assignment to carry out.

# CHAPTER THREE

## *Prized Gem*

*She is more precious than rubies and all the things you can desire are not to be compared to her.* Proverbs 3:15

The diamond is the purest gemstone. Out of all the diamonds mined in this world, only about 25 percent of them are considered gem quality. In history, diamonds always symbolized wealth, strength, and purity and only the kings and queens were permitted to adorn themselves with them. The kings and the men of royalty preferred to wear the diamonds so that their onlookers would be captivated in the sparkling radiance of the stone. And still, in the world today, everyone wants to be 'iced-up' or blinged out.

Diamonds are everywhere. In rings, watches, bracelets, and now even in teeth. They are still highly valued in the world and no other stone is as precious as the King of Gems. If you own any diamonds, they will probably outlast you and become the oldest thing you will ever own. Except for a trace of impurities, the stone is mostly made up of carbon. Carbon is the chemical element fundamental to all existence of life.

## FUNDAMENTAL TO LIFE

At the fall of mankind, God cursed Adam and Eve after they had eaten from the forbidden tree in the midst of the garden. She had made a terrible mistake. I am sure Eve felt rejected and cursed by her Father, and then she had to face Adam every morning. Looking into his eyes knowing that she was the reason for their banishment out of the garden, I know it was difficult for Eve. I try to imagine God's words as he spoke, '*and I will greatly multiply thy sorrow and thy conception; in sorrow thou shalt bring forth children...*" (see Genesis 3:16).

Her spirit must have felt impure and she must have felt worthless to know that she would bring forth her children in sorrow. But I am sure that it was also bittersweet knowing that God would still forgive her and bless her womb with children. Oh, how great it must've been to not only carry one, but two – for Cain and Able were twins. *And Adam knew Eve his wife; and she conceived and bare Cain, and said, I have gotten a man from the Lord. And she again bare his brother Abel.* (Genesis 4:1-2)

We know that the word of the Lord did not return void. Eve's sorrow was acknowledged when Cain murdered his brother Abel. I also wonder if by knowing that God's words had preceded her child's death, if she got angry with the Lord? There must have been a time when Eve felt alone. Did she understand that God was creating something in her? Through her pain, her tears, and her prayers – I do believe that she was comforted. Just as God forgave Eve and blessed her womb with children, Adam forgave Eve, too. Although things had gotten rough for them both, Adam did not leave his wife's side. He cleaved to his wife, willing to make their marriage work. He had no choice! After all, this was who God had given him! He could not leave her in the wilderness alone. He remained there for her.

We live in a time where divorce statistics are at an alarming percentage, and especially in the church. Since the beginning of man and woman, God was between marriage unions; in fact I believe there is no marriage without God. A marriage should never just be between the bride and the groom, God must be the glue to hold them together. Adam recognized Eve's design as a helpmeet and he honored and treasured God's selection and was faithful. God was also faithful as he blessed them again. Just like the diamond, even with the impurities and sin of her past, God chose her to be a key element that was fundamental to life. God was making her into a prized gem.

*And Adam called his wife's name Eve because she was the mother of all living (Genesis 3:20).* Even as she bare another son, Seth, the Bible says that Eve spoke, *For God, said she, hath appointed me another seed instead of Abel, whom Cain slew* (Genesis 4:25).

Our God of more chances and new mercies knows just what you need and when you need it. If you missed your call long ago, remember that God will bless you with another chance. You may get off track in life, in your sins and impurities, as we are all imperfect, but God has a plan in there. God had a plan for Eve through her high-pressure stages. Even through the loss of a child Eve learned that God was still faithful. When the pain and high-pressure of the former is over and the new birth of the latter comes springing forth as new life, you'll know that His faithfulness is everlasting. You will trust him more with each trial, through every tribulation, and most of all you'll learn of His comfort and love. Although Eve conceived her children in sorrow, she gave birth to the gospel with the birth of her third son Seth. Through him men would come to know God (see Genesis 4:26).

## PURPOSE BY DESIGN

I remember being in a rough place for a very long time. I didn't know my purpose and I was living outside of the will of God for my life. We were brought up in the Baptist church, and as children my cousins and I used to hear our grandmother, Grandma Blossie, in the back room praying and speaking in tongues. I remember our laughter in response to hearing her speak in tongues. Back then I thought her behavior was funny. Sometimes, she'd catch the Holy Ghost and we'd think she was going to stomp a whole in the apartment floor! God bless her soul! My grandmother lived until the age of 91 until her passing on October 15, 2010. She was a strong woman in the Lord. I miss her presence greatly. Although I was baptized at an early age, sang in the adult choir at the age of 12, it wasn't until the year 1999 when God really began to visit me. Those visitations didn't come out of a good place, either.

Early in life, I had dreams to become the next R&B singer and as a child I spent most of my days locked away in my room creating. Whether it was writing books, poetry, songs, or recording songs with use of two tape recorders, I spent hours alone in my room nourishing my gifts and talents. Those years of creating and singing landed me record deal before I graduated from high school and soon I found myself in a whirlwind relationship with a record executive who was not my husband. As a matter of fact, he was someone else's and nobody could understand how bad I wanted out. I know what it feels like to be in bondage – even in a relationship, to be in a situation you don't want to be in, but feel like you can't get out. I was definitely in a rough, wilderness place. Your rough place is always the place where the enemy tries to find some way in and cause you to fear the unseen and the unknown. But God's word tells us that *God has not given you a spirit of fear, but of love, peace and a sound mind* (II Timothy 1:7).

It seemed as though everything that could go wrong, did go wrong. I went through cycles of cars breaking down, losing jobs, to being homeless with my two children at that time. Temporary employment was my crutch for many years. In fact, I did that for several years and I honestly thought that the cycle would not end.

Year after year, I went through what seemed to be the same seasons. I can remember never living at the addresses listed on my driver's license for very long. I didn't understand it at that time as we never do, but God was definitely processing me for something greater. During this particular rough season, I was unemployed for almost two years and depended upon an unemployment check to support me and my children – no doors were opening, only the doors of the church. That's where I spent my time, serving the Lord. I know what it feels like to have a heart for God, serve him in the church, but go home to a setting that doesn't reflect a life in Christ. I went from condemnation to conviction in my processing. I cried a lot and needed much prayer, too. There were no doors or jobs opening up at that time and my unemployment soon ran out. It had gotten so bad that I had to return back home to live with my mother and the man I was with, went back home to live with his wife.

It was during those rough times when I began to seek God with my whole being. Since I didn't have a job to go to, I cried out and poured myself into His Word daily, seeking strength and courage to step out on faith and move into His will for my life. Sometimes you may have to cry all the way through your high-pressure stages. God had to take me through that in order to get me alone so that he could deal with me in intimacy.

The rough place that I was in was one that I had created for myself. Sometimes the very thing that we pray and ask God to get us out of is the result of the wrong choices we make. I was entangled in a relationship that God never ordained for me. Now that I look back, I can see that it was during those times when God began to whisper to me gently in the midnight hour and I learned relationship with Him as He began to pour into me. I had begun to spend time in worship and you would never see me anywhere without my Bible. Those R&B songs turned into songs of inspiration and when I used to sing about the club, I was now singing about the gospel of Jesus Christ. That very relationship with the record executive became beneficial to me later in my own music endeavors and business pursuits.

You see God always takes those things that are meant for our harm and use them for our good (Romans 8:28). He was creating a diamond out of me through the pressure. He was faceting me. After I had been down for so long, God gave me the strength and the courage to step out on faith as a single mother of two in His will. I did get a job, vehicle, and before I knew it I had moved into my own place, leaving the past behind. Not saying that I didn't have some obstacles or other issues to overcome – because I did, but the best part about it was I knew the goodness of God and I knew that I could survive and make it through the wilderness with Him. As a matter of fact, I learned how to trust Him even more there. You see, I didn't get my relationship with God or get introduced to my purpose through being baptized in water at church when I was 12 or through my grandmother's praises, I can't even say it happened at church while I stood at the altar on a Sunday morning; but I can say that I did get it through my pressure and my pain.

We must all go through what His will and our choices require of us and sometimes high-pressure is a sign that you are called to change. This is when you experience those emotions that don't feel so good. It is also during this time when you decide to go into that secret place that you might begin to feel some opposition or rejection from those closest to you. These wilderness places can be very hard to dwell in, but in trusting the Lord and standing on His word, we can begin to move higher into the fullness of what God has for us. Yes, it can become uncomfortable and almost unbearable, but as you grow during those stages, you will become steadfast and unmovable in the process.

Right now, you may be feeling picked on instead of picked out and question why you have to go through what you're going through. You may not feel worthy enough or even saved enough. Fear may be your enemy and you may feel like you will never get to where God desires for you to be. The truth of the matter is God's plans always prevail. Sometimes he designs the pathway of life so that it will take us through the dark wilderness places in order for us to appreciate living in His light. You've got to come through it in order to get to it. He will work things out for your good and His glory! My story didn't end there, bless God, but it played a vital role in my becoming who I am today. Your story doesn't have to end in a rough season, either. Yes, going through can be rough, but God is ever mindful of you and He knows everything that you're faced with.

# Esther

*And who knows but that you have come to a royal position for such a time as this.* Esther 4:14

# CHAPTER FOUR

## A Miner's Delight

*It is the glory of God to conceal a thing; but the honor of kings to search out a matter.* Proverbs 25:2

I remember a certain man of God that was interested in courting me say, *"How can I find you if you're hiding?"* That question was very profound to me. I intentionally had my guards up after not being in a relationship for a number of years and I myself was seeking God for a Word about this pursuer because I was adamant that he was not the man that God had sent to find me. However, with his question I realized that sometimes women tend to hide after experiencing so much pain in previous relationships that sometimes we make it difficult to be found after our processing is over.

We hide behind our jobs and our careers or our children and ministries and are not in place to be found – on purpose! So many women have decided that they no longer want to wait for husbands for their own personal reasons, resulting in a large number of women being the head's of their household's. They are going on with their lives and are not positioned for 'he who finds' to discover them. I didn't know how to answer his question, but I knew that if he were the right man he would have recognized his find, not categorizing me among the hidden still!

So, if you're among the unmarried, like me - while that miner is being tedious in his search for us, we must also remain patient in our waiting to be found. Just as that miner knows the general area to search for his find – trust that God knows who to send to find you. But you must be in that special place. A miner knows that he can't find a rough diamond in an obscure place that doesn't produce quality gems. Since diamonds are created under special conditions, the miner must be knowledgeable in where to search for the rough. He's not going to go searching for a rhinestone when his heart is set on a diamond. He knows he has to go to a special place for this delight.

Once roughs are discovered and mined; the rocks must still be sorted, separated by their size, shape, color and other characteristics. Finding that special gemstone is not always an easy task among so many other roughs, but sometimes there are those that outshine the others.

A newly mined rough diamond looks more like a weathered piece of glass, unlike the polished gem we see on display behind the glass cases. Rough diamonds are not easy to mine. Hence, ladies you shouldn't make yourself so easily accessible! Not saying you should play hard to get, but you certainly shouldn't be an easy catch, either. Men love challenges and some challenges are often depicted as an obstacle course – Amen! The whole entire process of diamond searching can be not only challenging but a dangerous one. Did you know that almost 300 tons of coal needs to be blasted, crushed and processed just to yield one diamond? These precious gems are the delight of a miner, regardless of how dangerous the process can be – he knows that he just can't look in any kind of place for it. He knows that mining is a tedious process and he understands that he must be patient and in his search efforts, he just may find a gem in the rubble.

## DIVINE ESCORT SERVICE

God has the greatest escort service on Earth. He is the best in the business of putting together husbands and wives. Oftentimes, when we marry out of our own selfish reasons outside of God's will and we tend to have issues in our unions, but God knows who will take you into their arms, love you and treat you with the utmost respect. I'm certainly not saying there won't be trying and difficult times, or times when you can't stand one another, but the true man that God has for you will recognize you as a diamond. You are to be cherished and treasured and you do not want to wind up in the wrong hands. God is such a gentleman to His diamonds that he desires to make sure we get to where we need to be by way of His escort service.

Eve was escorted to her husband. She was brought to him. God did not bring Adam to Eve. How many times have you heard *"Girl, when I find my husband"*... Perhaps that is your popular quote. Well, while you're looking, God has sat down, crossed His arms and is waiting on you to be still so he can position you to be sought out, like a diamond in the rough. Oftentimes we are going in the wrong direction in our own efforts. When you allow him to connect you with the best suitable miner, there is always a blessing in it.

Even Esther was escorted to the king's palace. She was brought unto the king's house by her uncle Mordecai. Some of us are being escorted and think God is being hard on us because we have not reached our destination, but if we look at the meaning of the escort – an escort does not normally accompany a person on short walks. An escort is defined as a body of persons or a single person accompanying another or others for protection, guidance, or courtesy. They are a safeguard or protection on a journey. If you are disconnected from your escort service, you lack the protection and guidance on your journey and you could end up marrying the wrong person. Let the Holy Spirit be your escort service. Let God guide you into the pathway of the person searching for you.

## 4 C's: THE CUT

When buying that perfect diamond becomes the main priority of the consumer, he knows that he doesn't want just anything. He not only wants beauty, but he also wants quality and the one gem that he will treasure forever. The consumer wants to know if their chosen gem is of good substance. If you know anything about diamonds, then you know about the 4 C's: *Cut, Color, Clarity, and Carat*. The right combination of all these categories can produce the perfect diamond.

When it comes to the diamond it's all about the cut. Out of the 4 C's, it is the *Cut* that is the key to unlocking the fiery sparkle. The cut is the faceting, the design of the diamond and it is oftentimes what allures or attracts the onlookers. When the diamond is cut, light is gathered within the diamond and then sent back out in an array of fire and brilliance. The beauty of the diamond only shows after processing, and can only be brought out by the diamond cutter through a process called *cleaving* or sawing. This is done to separate the original rough into a smaller more workable piece. When the diamond cutter cuts the workable piece in order to create the outline and shape of the new stone, he uses another diamond. Because a diamond is the hardest surface known to man, the diamond cutter must use another diamond to cut the original rough. A diamond saw, oiled with a combination of diamond dust and olive oil is used on the surface of the raw gem. The gem itself must be greased instead of wet. Water is used to wash away non-diamond particles, because water will not stick to the stone.

Isn't that how God desires us to be when we first come to him covered in layers of mess? He wants us to be a workable piece, and practically in pieces! He wants us on the potter's wheel – able to be shaped, fashioned and transformed. Like iron sharpening iron, we need another diamond in our life to lead us by example. We need Godly examples of not only women, but men as well in our midst during our processing.

The cut is a complicated process, but it also determines the diamond's unique beauty. The diamond cutter must be precise in the way he cuts the gem, because the wrong cut can ruin the whole diamond. Due to the crystal structure of the diamond, if it is cut wrong – its natural planes or lines of weakness can be split, however it never splits jagged or irregular. It always separates neatly along the lines. Diamond cutters take advantage of cleavage in preparation for a cut.

Once the diamond cutter has the rough at a workable piece, he begins to grind away the edges, in a process called *bruting,* providing the outline and the shape of the new stone. When looking at our journey in Christ, we sometimes do not welcome this pruning and broken stage. In fact, we resist the threshing floor process. God has to grind away the rough edges of our lives, even those edges that have surrounded our hearts. God desires to reshape them to fit His image. He also sees the potential of your beauty within and has even placed some gifts and talents for you to use in the advancement of His kingdom on Earth, He has to grind away the comfort of our comfort zones in order for us to move forward.

Many people will look upon you in those rough times and seasons where you're experiencing a tremendous amount of pain from life's cuts. You just have to remember that God has fashioned you and when you remain in His care, when your heart is shattered, the cuts will be so perfect that he will use it to continue fashioning you to fulfill His purpose in your life. There may be times when you may have to experience cuts in life that seem to split your very being. Be careful who prays for you, who you allow to speak into your life, and who you share your vision with. Some cuts are good, but you don't want the wrong person handling you and cutting you fatally.

It is the cut that unlocks your brilliance! This is what makes you different and those cuts create that brilliant sparkle you are to inherit as a diamond. What cut will be that one that will be used to bring out your fire in the Lord? Will it be a negative diagnosis from the doctor? Losing your job or maybe issues in your relationship? What cut would ultimately bring out your glow? It would be nice if we could determine our own cuts, but the diamond cutter, our Lord the Master Gemologist – knows what cut you need. He is the one with the vision of the perfect cut in mind. You just have to trust that His judgment will be in your best interest. He knows that he'd have to cut you so perfectly so that he could reflect His brilliance through you, and you will send that light back out into the world.

After the diamond cutter completes the outline and the faceting of the diamond it is then sent through a boiling process to remove dust and any oil. Once it is polished, it is then considered finished. It is interesting that this beauty by design is not a beautiful process. It is quite brutal to say the least. Sometimes the finished product blinds us and we don't see what it took for that diamond to go through to achieve the end result we see in elegant showcases. By the time we see the beauty the stone has come from ruin to royalty and has suffered at the hands of many.

## QUEEN OF GEMS

We have this young beautiful woman named Esther that is standing in the midst of a beauty contest waiting to be handpicked among many other maidens. All the maidens in attendance had heard the news that the king had released his wife Queen Vashti and he was looking for a new wife. Esther was among many beautiful women. Different shapes, sizes and shades of color, but we know that the king ultimately chose her because she pleased him. More than just her outer beauty gave her favor, but something he saw within her made him decide to make her his queen. She had won his favor, but how? Had the king already seen the gem that Esther was before he brought her into his palace? Not only did she have captivating beauty, but her name is derived from the Persian word for star, one of our natural sources of light. No wonder she was able to dazzle in the king's eyes and outshine the others.

Although Esther was chosen by the king, she still had to endure more processing. His decision to marry her didn't land her an immediate occupancy on the throne. She was immediately given things for purification, seven handmaidens, bridesmaids as I like to think of them, and she was placed under the care of Hegai, the keeper of women (See Esther 2:8-9). The king speedily gave her the things that belonged to her for purification. This man saw something in her and he was not slow about making preparations for them to become one. The king did not wait five years to come to a conclusion about who was going to share the throne with him. As my best friend would often say, "It doesn't take a whole day to recognize sunshine!"

Immediately, he provided her with her *beauty treatments and special food* (Esther 2:9). She had to complete *twelve months of beauty treatments prescribed for the women, six months of oil and myrrh and six with perfumes and cosmetics* (NIV) (see 2:12). The first thing that stood out to me was that he immediately gave to her, he provided her with.

Ladies, these are attributes that we should be looking for in a man. And I am certainly not saying you need him to give you anything – but you definitely want to see if he is a giver or a taker. You want someone that is going to be able to add to you and not take from you – at all. Especially if he is just your boyfriend or the man you're courting. Do not allow him to continue to take from you if he is not giving or providing you with anything. If you are in a relationship or have been in one for years and you live together unmarried – there are some issues to address. But we'll discuss those at a later time. The king immediately made provisions for Esther to become his wife. Granted, he had some things to prepare for her and to clean up with Queen Vashti, but he immediately became the provider for Esther – even though it would be a year later that they married.

CHAPTER FIVE

# The Princess Cut

*Many daughters have done virtuously, but thou excellest them all.* Proverbs 31:29

There had to be hundreds, maybe thousands of beautiful handmaidens competing to become queen. I'm sure they were fair and beautiful by the number, many probably princesses from other palaces. Esther had favor. Her beauty was valuably a cut above the rest, but it was her divine purpose that caused favor to cover her. In the midst of all the beauty and purification treatments, she never revealed her nationality to her bridesmaids or to the king. She had to make sure that her processing was complete, so that when the time was come for her to be brought into the courts as his queen; she would have flair and sparkle.

I'm sure Esther wasn't happy for that entire year of processing in the king's palace. I'm sure she bumped heads from time to time with Hegai, her keeper and wanted to drop out of the competition. The fasting, praying, the consecration – all those things she needed for her purification, but I'm certain her flesh warred against her spirit at times. But God was reshaping her to fit His image; he had to grind away some things off Esther, placing His glory upon her for the advancement of His kingdom on Earth.

Once Esther became queen, she saved her nation through her God-given favor with her husband. She was a heroine in her day, strategically placed among the fairest to be chosen and handpicked by the king in order that she may free her own people from the snares of death. What if she has been wrapped in the spirit of fear during the twelve months of purification, or trampled by the spirit of intimidation? Esther could've easily stepped out of line during the competition and returned home with her uncle Mordecai, but she maintained her composure through it all and she came out shining like the diamond that she was.

Esther made it through her processing. She endured the competition's whole year of waiting during her cutting process, and when the final cut was made, Esther was the one standing beside the king. *"He set the royal crown upon her head, and made her queen instead of Vashti"* (Esther 2:2).

# CHAPTER SIX

# You Are Brilliant

*Thou art fair, my love; there is no spot in thee.*
Song of Solomon 4:7

Not only do diamonds come in different shapes and sizes, but they also come in many colors. In fact, even your diamond that appears to have no color has color. Colorless diamonds are rare. You have your white, yellow, blue, and even pink diamonds. Diamonds come in every color of the rainbow! Color is caused by impurities and trace elements within their crystal structure, which happens during the high pressure stage. These structural distortions causes tints which gives color to the diamond, categorized as fine color, top color, or fancy color. However, out of all the 4 C's the *Color* is what affects the *value* of the rough.

## 4 C's: THE COLOR

The *Color* of a diamond has a dynamic impact on the appearance of the stone. With the perfect *Cut*, a colorless diamond can reflect light into a spectrum of hues. This is the flicker of 'fire' within the gemstone that is released to onlookers. The more color that is noticeable in the diamond, the less light is produced. It is the cut and the color that creates the fiery brilliance that we see in many diamonds. The less color you have in the gem, the more brilliant and more expensive it is.

Color can affect the value of a stone by hundreds, even thousands of dollars. Gemologists evaluate color in diamonds to determine its value. The difference in color usually means the higher in value, but the color's impact on beauty is a personal matter. In order to effectively complete this evaluation, the stone is compared to what are called master stones. More interestingly, color is graded by the human eye, which is best for grading and only during the morning when vision is sharper. Graders only work when they are only in good health giving their insight on hues, tones, and saturation.

What do people see when they look upon you? Do they see your imperfections, flaws and shortcomings? Will they recognize you by your past and sins? No matter how valuable you are, there will always be those that will look upon you with their human eyes and grade you according to what they see. I am so glad that God looks upon us in a way that man doesn't. God looks at the heart, while man looks at the outer appearance (1 Samuel 16:7). Man will look upon us and grade us because of what we look like, not recognizing that what's on the inside counts. Man will look upon us and stereotype us because of what outfit we have on or depending on what shoes we wear on our feet. If we do not wear the most expensive labels or designers then we seemingly don't fit the bill. The Lord told Samuel not to look at the appearance. Have you ever met someone that appeared to have it all together, but really did not? They may have seemed like they would be the nicest person, but once they opened their mouth, you discovered that their heart was hard and ugly.

The world will judge you by your failures, your shortcomings, flaws and all. I am reminded by Tyler Perry's movie, *For Colored Girls* where each woman wore a color that described her personality in the role that she played. The color that she wore depicted her value. One of the actresses wore white, which showed her on-screen personality as one that was pure, holy, and sanctified. Another one wore red, which showed us her fiery, domineering personality. If there was a color to depict your value, what would it be?

Though your sins may be as scarlet, you have a savior that died for you and your sins have been blotted out! *Though your sins are like scarlet, they shall be white as snow; though they are red like crimson, they shall be as wool* (Isaiah 1:18).

How valuable was that red bloodstain over the door posts at Passover! *Woman of Brilliance*, don't let your sins devalue you. It costs more to carry the stain of sin, because the wages of it are death! Let God's love remove the color of crimson and scarlet from your appearance that you are able to stand before him without a spot, colorless and white as snow, because it does matter - your sins affect your value, it is critical to your worth. What is your degree of colorlessness? Do you appear to have it altogether outwardly? Can you put a price on your worth? The Bible says it is priced far above rubies – so it must be diamond!

How thankful I am to know that God has removed and blotted out all of my transgressions to brilliance! I can be a diamond that appears colorless to the human eye, shameless and blameless before Him.

# Hannah

*For your shame ye shall have double; and for confusion they shall rejoice in their portion: therefore in their land they shall possess the double: everlasting joy shall be unto them.*
Isaiah 61:7

# CHAPTER SEVEN

## Hello Beauty, Goodbye Ashes

*And she said, Let thine handmaid find grace in thy sight. So the woman went her way, and did eat, and her countenance was no more said.* I Samuel 1:18

The beauty of the stone is captivating, but even the most precious stones have nature's fingerprint. I call it God's fingerprint. Those fingerprints are the natural inclusions within the diamond such as black or white marks, which are found in many stones. It is these marks that determine *Clarity*, one of the 4 C's.

## 4 C's: THE CLARITY

They are something like a birthmark. At some point in formation, those inclusions occur. In the previous chapters we talked about how the perfect cut and degree of colorless can unlock the fiery brilliance of the stone, determining value – well clarity is a term that is used to describe the absence of blemishes in the diamond.

Even while going through your rough place, there will be some things that will remain as fingerprints on your journey. No one is free from life's naturally occurring inclusions. These inclusions vary from woman to the next, but we all have some things that we have to deal with and face. However you choose to label them – natural inclusions, scars, or wounds, what you been through; rape, drugs, or abuse – God has a plan that includes your inclusions. Sometimes these naturally occurring inclusions become burdens in your life.

Burdens that you carry along with you on your journey that ultimately become a part of your testimony as you continue to walk by faith. The pain of coming into your worth, 'far above rubies' can be tremendous. This can sometimes cause you to question the plan that God has for your life. Endless cycles, countless tears, unconquered fears and apprehension attempt to become your daily mindset. You may even doubt that all the pain is even worth the reward in the end. But, *Woman of Brilliance*, you are going to have to endure a lot of pain in order to birth out that prized gem within you. Your pain is prophetic. It's all about your longsuffering. You must go through it. I don't care if you were born with a silver spoon in your mouth, you will still have to go through the pain in giving birth to something. Yes, there will be troubles, but God didn't promise us that we would be free from trials and tribulations. The psalmist says, *Trouble don't last always.*

Many are the afflictions of the righteous, so know that because he chose you out of the ashes, you were handpicked to be custom-designed for a specific purpose. How wonderful it is to possess such brilliance and in depth quality! You came out of layers and layers of stuff, to be elevated and found and now you are here – ready to be designed with vision, adorned with flair, and polished to perfection. The amount of pressure endured is somewhat inconceivable. Nobody knows what you had to endure; nobody knows the cost of your oil!

Hannah was one of the wives of Elkanah. She had her own natural inclusions that clothed her with the spirit of heaviness. Hannah was barren. Hannah and her husband were unable to conceive any children together. Although it was custom for men to have multiple wives, I'm sure that it still bothered Hannah to be left home alone while her husband was with Penninah. She had children of her own and would provoke and taunt Hannah. She would make her feel worthless. In the Hebrew society, one of the greatest tragedies that could befall a woman was to be barren. One thing the Hebrew people knew was that children were blessings from God, a heritage (Psalm 127:3).

Although Elkanah did not have children with Hannah, she remained the favored of the two. Penninah realized that she was not the favored wife and was very jealous of Hannah.

Her jealousy was so personal that Hannah was bitterly upset and would grieve so badly that she became depressed and would not eat. The enemy of her spirit tormented her year by year she was provoked sore by Penninah. She was at the end of her rope. Hannah's pressure had mounted and a volcano was waiting to erupt and give birth to something life changing.

## JUST BECAUSE HE LOVES ME

Hannah's degree of clarity was not among that of a choice gem. She thought that Penninah was a complete woman, by being able to conceive children. But, Penninah was far from a gem. By her actions and her attitude she resembled more of the likeness to a rhinestone, which is nothing more than glass; or a cubic zirconium which has less sparkle and brilliance than a diamond.

Elkanah and Hannah had a special relationship that I relate to an affair of love, or as the French say it, affaire d'amour. The word affair is defined as anything done or to be done which requires action or effort not only limited to love, but in business, concerns, or other interests. They had a love affair as husband and wife. In observing Elkanah and Hannah there had to have been some reasonable amount of effort on Elkanah's part because he had to keep both women happy. But in Hannah he gave her more to let her know his feelings for her over Penninah. How great are the things that love does for us! All because he loved her, he gave her the worthy, double portion.

He looked upon her and saw no flaw, and chose her out of many. Colorless and pure, like the most valued diamond on display, he loved her perfectly. Elkanah had an intimate love affair with his wife. Love is described as a strong or passionate affection for a person. It is a personal attachment or a deep affection for a person and is an enduring emotional regard. The Bible did not say because she was prettier, or because her bank account was bigger, or because she wore all the designer clothes; but only because he loved her, he gave her the biggest portion. In today's day and time, we would think that Penninah would have gotten the biggest portion because she had the children. What a man in love won't give to the woman he loves!

Women should consider Hannah's story, especially those who settle with being 'the other woman'. I've heard far too many men say that they love more than one woman. I've heard it from the reality show polygamists, to that 'single' guy who approaches you with interest, but has a 'boo' on the side. Yes, how many of us have run into the one who thinks that you're willing to settle with him, while he loves and is involved with someone else. Take into consideration Elkanah, he could easily take this position and say that he loved two women. But once again, the Bible is clear to let us know that he loved Hannah more. So many women of today have settled with knowing that their man is in love with someone else. Someone will always suffer and end up with the shorthand of the stick. That man will always love one more than the other and I pray that you are not on the shorthand of receiving. Hannah ended up getting the greater portion of the relationship, although Penninah had all the children.

You don't have to settle anymore. There is a love unfeigned in your midst! Some of you are in your 'just because he loves me season'. It doesn't matter what you've done or are still doing, some of you are about to come into the blessing of the Lord that makes rich and adds no sorrow, just because Jesus loves you. He gives us gifts without repentance – so it is nothing that you have or will do that will keep you from the blessing that God has to give out of his love.

## LOVER OF YOUR SOUL

*Then said Elkanah her husband to her, Hannah, why weepest thou? And why eatest thou not? And why is thy heart grieved? Am not I better to thee than ten sons?* I Samuel 1:8

Although her husband was more attentive and supportive to her, there were some things that Hannah desired that her husband could not give to her. If you are not familiar with the story, one year while they ate in Shiloh with other priests such as Eli, he asked her why she cried. He wanted to know what caused her grief in the most intimate place inside of her – her heart. But Hannah had another intimate love affair with someone who already knew that she desired to conceive. Elkanah wanted to know why she didn't eat and why she was downhearted. But Hannah rose from the table, with bitterness in her soul and prayed unto the Lord as she wept. Although Elkanah desired to know his wife's innermost, God already knew why her tears fell.

*And she vowed a vow, and said, O Lord of hosts, if thou wilt indeed look on the affliction of thine handmaid, and remember me, and not forget thine handmaid, but wilt give unto thine handmaid a man child, then I will give him unto the Lord all the days of his life.* I Samuel 1:11

Hannah prayed from her heart, moving nothing but her lips as the scripture tells us. Her voice was not heard. She made a vow to the Lord in her heart and it was interesting that Eli believed she was drunk. She confessed that she was not drunk, but a woman of a sorrowful spirit that had poured out her soul before the Lord. We must be careful when trying to gauge a person in processing. People will believe you to be drinking from the cup of loneliness, brokenness, financial lack and depression. They judge your tears, believing they indicate too much being taken in, when more times than not – our tears happen in our pouring out to God. Eli the priest sent her away in peace and touched and agreed with her that God granted her petition.

All Hannah needed was someone to believe with her. Penninah had opposed her for so long and her own husband believed he was enough for her, but as Hannah wept and made her request known and Eli watched her in prayer - the Lord was in the midst of them (Matthew 18:19). As Eli sent her away in peace, she did eat and her countenance wasn't sad anymore. The next morning they rose early, worshipped the Lord and the Lord remembered Hannah when her husband lay with her.

*Wherefore it came to pass, when the time was come about after Hannah had conceived, that she bare a son, and called his name Samuel, saying, because I have asked him of the Lord.* I Samuel 1:20

Although Hannah had an intimate love affair with her husband, she had an even greater intimacy with love, itself. Even though she had naturally occurring inclusions that may have temporarily distorted her degree of clarity, she was still loved by Elkanah and given double portions over Penninah. By recognizing that there were just some things that Elkanah could not give her, she made her request specific to the Lord, and her request was granted.

We all have some natural inclusions that we have to contend with that may affect our degree of clarity, oftentimes making us feel unworthy and less wanted. Some blemishes are related to the original rough, but most are due to the result of the environment the jewel has encountered since it was uncovered. Diamonds with fewer inclusions are rare and greater in price anyway. There is no surprise that many diamonds have inclusions, scratches, blemishes, air bubbles, or non-mineral material – look at all the pressure they have to go through as God is making them!

What will you do with your inclusions? Will you continue to cover them up and weep while carrying the inclusion as a burden or will you pour out your request to the Lord like Hannah did? Hannah's son Samuel would be given to the Lord as Hannah had vowed. He would know and hear the Lord at an early age, and Samuel even ministered before the Lord under Eli's leadership. He would become one of the prophets of old as covered in his two books in the Bible. Not only did God cover the natural inclusion once, but he also remained faithful to Hannah and rewarded her faithfulness later, giving her three more sons and two daughters. God took her closed womb and opened up her mourning into joy with new birth.

What once may have placed her in an isolated place brought her to a wealthy place. Your clarity is that of a prized gem and after you have poured out your all to God, the spots or blemishes that may have been obvious or apparent to the world are now out of sight. No longer will they see your downfalls, they will only see His glory. Many are the inclusions of a life under pressure. Low self-esteem, scars of bondage, and the bruises of learning how to crawl and walk after being defeated for so long may be apparent at first, but you will even survive your scars and even they will be made over. The cutting away, the bruting away, the grinding away of all your imperfections and everything that was not like him, was to ultimately bring out who you really are – not what people see or by what you've been through. When God gets through with you, no one will even recognize you in all of your brilliance.

# Joanna

*Thine eyes did see my substance, yet being unperfect…*
Psalm 139:16

# CHAPTER EIGHT

# Substance of the Stone

*And Joanna the wife of Chuza Herod's steward, and Susanna, and many others, which ministered unto him of their substance.* Luke 8:2

Do you remember the first time you actually laid your eyes on a diamond? Maybe it was the day your husband proposed to you with your ring in a beautifully gift-wrapped box. Or maybe you have shared the joy of an engagement with a girlfriend, longing to ask that big question that we all ask, *"How many carats is it"?*

## 4 C's: THE CARAT

The *Carat,* another one of the 4 C's, is the unit of weight or the size of the gemstone, not to be confused with karat (the method of determining the purity of gold). It is the importance, emphasis, or the substance of the stone. The weight of the stone also determines its value. The larger diamonds are uncovered less often than smaller ones. They are also rare and have greater value per carat as the price goes up with the size. Even in choosing a diamond for a loved one, the importance of the size is probably heavily based on how important that loved one is to you.

What is the substance of the weight that you carry, gem? What is your value? As a *Woman of Brilliance*, you may find yourself trying to determine your place and purpose in life. You may have some unfulfilled dreams and desires that you want to accomplish and step out on faith to achieve. Maybe you want to go back to school for that business degree you have put off decades ago. You may even know or feel as if God is calling you to ministry. As a disciple of Christ will you be able to carry out the weight of the call to follow? Can you walk with Jesus, knowing His longsuffering and the weight of His call?

Jewish tradition did not allow women to study the law with a rabbi. So these women who were seen in the midst of the Messiah probably followed him against all odds. Many people were probably offended as a loving and compassionate Jesus crossed all religious barriers by inviting the women to sit and break bread with him. He encouraged them to sit at His feet. *And she had a sister called Mary, which also sat at Jesus' feet, and heard his word* (Luke 10:39).

They were fit for service and fit for ministry. They remained supportive and faithful, always being there until the end. They left their homes, families, and possessions just as the twelve disciples did. When Jesus saw Simon and Peter fishing in the Sea of Galilee all he said to them was *"Follow me and I will make you fishers of men"* (Matthew 4:19). The Bible says they straightway left their nets and followed him. Without understanding, reason, complaint or a thought, they immediately followed.

If you were a woman in that time, leaving your comfort zone to step out on faith and follow Jesus, what would you give to him? I imagined that I was among the women standing in the midst of Jesus desiring to minister to him out of my substance. What would I give? Would I break open my alabaster box and give my oil? Would I wash His feet with my tears and my hair? In that time, Jewish women rarely had control of much money, so these women provided whatever they could to assist or simply help or show gratitude. Helping was programmed and embedded within them and all these women named by the disciples had something that they wanted to give to the Giver. I am sure there were others who had nothing to give, so they gave themselves to him in loyalty and faithfulness in service.

## DIAMOND DISCIPLESHIP

The disciples of Jesus recorded in their writings that there were also women surrounding the life of Jesus. We don't know how many traveled with Jesus and the disciples throughout His ministry, but in the three books of Jesus' life and ministry the names of the women differ, but the fact that there were many never changes.

In the book of Matthew, he mentions that *many women followed Jesus from Galilee, ministering to him from afar off* (Matthew 27:55-56). By name, Matthew recalls Mary Magdalene, Mary the mother of James and Joses, and the mother of Zebedee's children. Mark mentions them, as well as Salome. Luke called them certain women, only mentioning by name, Mary Magdalene, Joanna the wife of Chuza, and Susanna (Luke 8:2). Who were these certain women that ministered to Jesus out of their substance? I must say I liked the way Luke used His words. He described them as certain, which means simply having no doubt. These women were sure, confident and indisputable when it came to their decision to follow Jesus and take up their cross in a life of ministry. They didn't care what was not permitted in the law of that time regarding women; they were dedicated and unfailing to their undying commitment. These women of certainty remained steadfast and unmovable and well able to carry the weight of their ministry.

What is the character of a woman that follows Jesus? Matthew and Mark noted that these women ministered to Jesus, but Luke described them as those that ministered unto him of their substance. One translation says it this way, "These women were helping support them out of their own means." These women traveled with Jesus and His disciples throughout His teachings, contributing to their needs out of their own resources – probably preparing and serving meals, providing water, and clean clothes.

Isn't it a wonderful thing that God had specifically chosen and prepared these women especially to fill this role in Jesus' life, death, and resurrection? This was their purpose by design and their destiny. Much like anyone who decides to live a life of ministry for Jesus, I am sure they suffered because of their certainty. Those family members that were left in Jerusalem who did not believe in Jesus' teachings probably thought the women were foolish to leave their homes and their livelihood to follow Christ.

CHAPTER NINE

# Carrying Your Weight

*For our light affliction, which is but for a moment, works for us a far more exceeding and eternal weight of glory.*
2 Corinthians 4:17

One woman that drew me in was Joanna. I desired to know more about her because she was the only one mentioned to have been married. She was the wife of Chuza, Luke states. Chuza was the manager of Herod Antipas' household, some may interpret Chuza as just being Herod Antipas' butler. Chuza was a steward of a wealthy ruler, which probably meant he was well off too. I am sure he shared some of Herod's wealth, being the manager of the king's household. If we remember Herod the Great, Antipas' father, he was the ruler of the Jewish Palestine under Rome who sent out men to search for a baby Jesus. God spoke to Joseph warning him about Herod's desire to destroy the child. Herod the Great murdered all the children of Bethlehem from the age two and under.

Now, we have Joanna, married to a man who runs the household for Herod Antipas and Joanna has chosen to follow Christ. Herod Antipas was not much different from his father.

He also supported Jesus' crucifixion and delivered John the Baptist's head on a platter for his stepdaughter Salome (who is also mentioned to follow Jesus – Glory!). How could this be? How did the woman, married to the man who works for the opposition of Christ come to leave the side of her husband to not only follow, but dedicate her life, strength and substance to become not just a minister, but a servant of Jesus Christ?

Isn't it like our marvelous God to turn the kingdom of Herod into means to support the ministry of Jesus Christ? Although the Bible doesn't give great detail about the reason why Joanna decided to take up her cross and support Jesus, I am almost certain she heard that he was leaving Galilee to teach to the multitudes and immediately made the decision – whether she had to leave Chuza or not. Perhaps Chuza spent more time managing Herod's household that he had forgotten to love his wife. With nothing more than a mustard seed of faith and the garments on her back she decided to follow him. She was among the many women to take a hold of the plow and never looked back at their lives.

Can you imagine these certain women meeting wherever they could as Jesus would settle to teach, they would stand afar off, by the well as they pitched water they would marvel over the words he spoke to the multitude. Perhaps in their plight, he taught a word fitly spoken into their hearts. Joanna and the other certain women followed Jesus from the beginning to the end and thereafter. Jesus' earthly life was taken and he was laid in the tomb and the next morning these certain women, still using their own means, prepared spices for the body. Their hearts were fixed as they remained faithful even after Jesus' death. They had gone to the tomb and found that the stone was rolled away.

*Now upon the first day of the week, very early in the morning, they came unto the sepulcher, bringing the spices, which they had prepared, and certain others with them. It was Mary Magdalene, and Joanna, and Mary the mother of James, and other women that were with them, which told these things unto the apostles. And their words seemed to them as idle tales, and they believed them not* (Luke 24:1, 10-11).

Jesus valued women. These women were gifts to him and His disciples. Men need the gifts, insight, and observations of the women in their lives. Godly women compliment Godly men, in ministry, work, and in services. Jesus cast down the walls of division between genders. He included them in His life and ministry. The moment Jesus asked you to follow Him, you had something to render. There was something that He saw in you – even at your lowest low that made Him approach you in spirit and ask you to follow Him. I don't know what your substance is or how you weigh it. However you measure your carat, continue to follow and support Christ's ministry, your husband, your children, your business or career. Remember that your substance is in your service. Know that there is value in your substance.

# O Gomer

*And I will sow her unto me in the earth, and I will have mercy upon her that had not obtained mercy.* Hosea 2:23

# CHAPTER TEN

## *Certified in Quality*

*Hath not my hand made all these things?* Acts 8:50

Selecting a diamond can be a difficult task for anyone and most of the time, the consumer desires some sort of guarantee in his newly purchased stone. They want to know that their chosen gem was not just a good selection, but that it was good in quality. Although they may use the 4 C's *(Cut, Color, Clarity, Carat)* to determine which jewel would be suitable, they also have the option of obtaining a certificate that verifies the gems quality.

The gemologist initiates the diamond report by judging the quality of the stone and documents in great descriptive detail the internal and external characteristics of the diamond. The report is the blueprint for the diamond, or its birth certificate and has specific information relating to the diamond noted and shows the general features of the stone and details the course or results of a process. Each diamond is given an identification number and details a diamond's Depth,

Fluorescence, Measurements, Polish Detailing, Proportion, Symmetry and other information that the gemologist would want to comment about the stone. It also lists the instruments that were used to examine the stone, and describes and grades the diamond. This report is very detailed as it also shows a diagram, descriptive of the diamond's shape, cut, clarity, color, and plots the internal and external characteristics of the diamond. On the diagram, the diamond is plotted with different symbols for the different characteristics. Plotting is done to identify the diamond, document the condition and characteristics of it, and it serves to support and justify the clarity grade.

## REVEALING THE PLOT

If God were to have a certificate of quality report on you, what would it detail? How would you handle the plots or circumstances that God may use to blueprint you? Just like the gemologist needs a diagram to serve as a blueprint for the diamond, God often needs some sort of diagram to grade our 'quality'. He sometimes uses plots and situations in our lives to identify us. He needs to know whom we love and serve and he may send us through a trial or a test, so he can know for sure that we belong to him and he is ours. It ultimately tries our faith. Sometimes it is these tests that we go through, where others in our circle may have to endure our processing as well.

In the book of Hosea, God gave word to Hosea to go and take a prostitute for a wife, along with her children. Can you imagine the pain and confusion that he must've felt when God spoke those words to him? Hosea probably desired to be married and someday have a family, but to marry a prostitute and take in her children as his own – I am sure that was not what he envisioned for himself. Obviously God must've made a mistake telling him to marry a prostitute and besides, what would everybody think when they saw them together? Hosea had to make a difficult decision, but he remained obedient as he had to trust that God's selection for him was best.

In faced with the decision to marry Gomer, wouldn't it have been nice if Hosea could've obtained a certificate from God verifying her quality or maybe some type of guarantee that she would remain faithful? I believe that God's word was enough for Hosea. God knew Gomer better than anyone else. He knew her depth, her measurements, her downfalls, her innermost, and most of all he knew her heart. I believe Hosea put his trust in God and made a decision that would ultimately change their lives.

## EYE OF THE BEHOLDER

Hosea took Gomer to be his wife as God had asked him to do and they conceived three children together and then something went wrong. Gomer was drawn back in the streets. Perhaps she felt that the married life was not for her so she gave into adultery, believing that her husband could not give her everything that she needed. Maybe the temptations of her past flooded her new life and swept her away back into its strong grasp. Gomer had been an unfaithful wife and Hosea's heart was broken.

As I read the scripture I imagined him going into prayer in the early hours of the morning seeking God about his word to marry her. It was difficult for Hosea who had faith, but was confused in his sorrow and pain, wondering why God had asked him to marry Gomer in the first place. It was even more difficult I'm sure, taking care of the children who were not his own when she disappeared. The scripture paints the picture of a man at his end, sending her children out in the night to find her, hoping that their presence would bring her home, but at the same time giving up altogether on their marriage. *"Plead with your mother, plead, for she is not my wife, neither am I her husband, let her be therefore put away.*

*And I will not have mercy on her children, for they be children of whoredoms." (Hosea 2:2, 4)*

Hosea probably questioned himself, unsure of his own ability to go on with the relationship, but Hosea continued to give her love. The Hebrew name Gomer means *completion.* Completion defined as *sound, wholesome, unimpaired, and finished and to be at an end.* How ironic to be so far from what God called her to be. Gomer was far from complete. God was still finishing her and making her into one of his jewels.

## BE THOU MADE WHOLE

I can see Gomer after finding herself next to a new stranger. Her children would cross her mind and she would suddenly feel guilt ridden and try to hide herself, but Gomer could not hide from God. She had a wonderful husband at home, but was bound by the spirit of prostitution. I wonder how many times God would try to reach Gomer. He would speak to her early in the morning in loving-kindness, but she would not hear his voice. On the inside she was not happy with herself. I am sure that she had thoughts of going home many times, desiring to be a whole woman, but rebelliously continued along her adulterous path becoming a slave to her lifestyle. She was in desperate need of a makeover.

Hosea's relationship with his wife really sketches the Biblical portrait of God's relationship with Israel and his love for us. God illustrates a picture of Israel chasing after her lovers. He describes how she will say, *"I will go back to my husband as at first, for then I was better off than now."* I could hear Gomer speak those words as she was being passed around from slave master to slave master, man to man. I could almost see her face as she stands in the cold, in line with other prostitutes for sale. Her children's faces flashing before her, as tears fall down her face in steady streams, she whispers the name of her faithful husband.

How many times have we run away from God's call for us to obey his will, and we end back up in the arms of a world that doesn't love us or care about us? For many of us, it was the arms of a man who didn't care about us. When God has been beckoning all along for us to come unto him and take on his easy yoke, giving him our heavy burdens.

## WELCOME YOUR WILDERNESS

Although Gomer was unfaithful, God had no intentions to leave her alone in her sin. The wonderful thing about God is that he always provides a way of escape, but sometimes we are so deep in the wilderness that it's hard to find our way out and we become so absorbed in our surroundings that we panic and focus on where we are in the situation, instead of him.

*Therefore, behold, I will allure her, and bring her into the wilderness and speak comfortably to her.* Hosea 2:14

Some of you are in your wilderness places right now and you're angry with God. You keep praying that he takes you out of your situation, position, or whatever else you are seeking the exit sign on. While you are angry and focused on your location in the wilderness, you won't even look up and notice that he has made this place especially for you.

I have found that it is in my wilderness places that I find such gratification in the presence of the Lord. I absolutely love it. It is where I open my word and the Holy Spirit opens my eyes to things and it is a time where God shares with me in intimacy. The wilderness gives me the opportunity to focus on God wholeheartedly, without distractions. It is my secret place, where I can simply indulge in his word, in his presence, and worship. It is the place made especially for you, where you are nourished, fed and satisfied. Let's make one thing clear - the flesh does not like the wilderness.

*And to the woman were given two wings of a great eagle, that she might fly into the wilderness, into her place, where she is nourished for a time, and times and a half, a time from the face of the serpent.* Revelation 12:14

Remember when you were growing up as a teen and you wanted to go to this party that somebody you knew was giving but you were on a punishment? Your parents told you to stay in your room and banned you from going to the party. Remember how bad you really wanted to go? Don't tell me I was the only one with a recollection! Just knowing so and so was going to be there tormented you. You wanted to be among all of your peers and your friends – and some of us even went as far as sneaking out of the house to get out of that wilderness place. The truth is, sometimes it gets that way in the spirit as well. We'd much rather be out of a place of isolation and in a place of comfort and companionship with other people.

You'd better get in your place of worship. A place where you can fly with your God-given eagle's wings and get nourished for some time out of the face of the devil. Welcome your wilderness and be glad in knowing that the devil can't mess with you there. Gomer had let her flesh get the best of her and she almost succumbed to her lifestyle, but God had not forgotten about her. God told Hosea to go and love her still according to the love of the Lord toward the children of Israel, even though she was an adulterous woman. God wanted Hosea to love his wife just as Christ loved the church with an Agape' love, a spiritual and boundless love unfeigned. It was hard to imagine that Hosea could even want Gomer back, after she had left home several times against the will of her husband, children and most importantly God.

Her blueprint was not that of a wife, but one of a prostitute. Hosea obeys the instruction of the Lord and went out to find her. I could see a picture of him praying before he left the house with the children, making them a promise in his heart that he would not return home without their mother. I could see him searching the streets to find her, calling out her name, hoping, wishing, and praying of a glimpse of her so he could run to her and embrace her and love back her self-esteem. He loved her and he wanted her back home with him and the children.

Welcome your wilderness today. Know that God has purpose in it. Even if you're on the wrong side of your purpose like Gomer was, God will send his unconditional love to save you. Even if you just feel like you're all alone and your home may be a place of isolation and wilderness, God will still allure you, he will still speak softly to you. He is creating something new inside of you and sometimes it is in those wilderness places where we take refuge in the secret place of the Most High and he shelters us from the enemy and feeds us under the shadow of his wing. Although the wilderness can be a place of loneliness and discomfort and it may even take us prayer and praise just to get through the rough places, I promise you that if you hold on for just a little while longer in your faith and don't give up, God will show up and show out for sure. Your life will receive a supernatural makeover, customized especially for you. Love will find a way!

# CHAPTER ELEVEN

# Purchased With a Price

*For ye are bought with a price; therefore glorify God in your body, and in your spirit, which are God's.* I Corinthians 6:20

Rough diamonds are displayed during selling sessions called 'sights'. These sights are by invite only and if the sight holders view a rough diamond that they like, they are able to cut the diamond right then and there and buy them, or they could sell some of the rough diamonds to smaller manufacturers. Once the polished gem is complete it is placed in the hands of someone who has the capabilities of further bringing out their beauty. This person takes the stone he has and dresses it by placing the stone in other pieces of jewelry such as a ring, bracelet, earrings, charms, or a pendant.

Hosea finally discovered where his wife was, learning that she had been sold into the slavery of prostitution. Can you imagine as Hosea walked into this exclusive sighting, barging his way through a crowd of people looking for Gomer? I'm sure there were so many lost women who had lost their identity in the process. No longer did they enjoy the lives they led. Many of the women were like lost little girls searching for love. After all, it was looking for love in the wrong places that had gotten them on someone's shopping list. Woman of God, whatever you do – whatever you endure, don't lose your identity in the process. Remember your likeness and your image is God's when you look in the mirror. You are the king's daughter, and not just any king – but The King of King, Lord of Lord's!

Hosea saw his wife and immediately felt compassion for her. I believe that at this point, Gomer had lost hope and was drowning in the sea of a sinful life. I'm sure she wanted to be at home with Hosea and the children very badly at this time, not knowing that her savior was already in her midst. Hosea went over to the seller of the prostitutes and began to reason with him regarding Gomer. He would purchase her for a price and take her home. He reasoned with the slave master and purchased Gomer from him for fifteen pieces of silver and one and one half of barley.

I can see Hosea racing through the crowd of people trying with all his might to get to her as fast as he could and rescue her. He wanted to let her know how beautiful she was inside and out and most importantly, how much he still loved her – even though she had been unfaithful. Can you imagine the look upon her face when she saw her husband? Although she may have been happy to see him, I am sure she was embarrassed and ashamed, but Hosea was filled with the unconditional love of God and disregarded the state that he found her in, after all it is love the covers a multitude of sins. Remember God's words he spoke to her spirit, *"Thou shalt abide with me for many days, though shalt not play the harlot, and thou shalt not be for another man, so will I also be for thee" (Hosea 3:3).*

      Hosea spoke prophetically into the spirit of his wife. He let her know that as long as she remained faithful to him he would always be faithful to her. He let her know that at home is where he desired her to be, abiding forever just as God desires for us as his children. God's mercy and grace over Israel was shown through Hosea's commitment and covenant with his wife and God has the same covenant with you. He will never leave you out there in your mess without alluring you in love to come back. Unfortunately, many don't listen or accept the plea of love and die in the wilderness by their own choice. I believe that after Hosea purchased her out of slavery that she then became whole and complete. Without an invite, Hosea walked into the enemy's territory and got back what was his. He was invited by God to an exclusive event and had come to take his wife home, clean her and dress her up and bring out her beauty.

Hosea had gotten his certificate of quality for his gem and not by the slave master or by anything that Gomer had done to demonstrate she was the number one pick. It was God who certified Gomer in quality. She had been through a rough season, but God had a miner to come and search her out of her sinful life. It is so like God in his tender love and mercies, that he searches us out in love. Although she went astray, she was welcomed back into the arms of one who could overlook her faults.

For many, Gomer was reported to be a prostitute, a woman of no value, and filth. The town probably wondered why Hosea continued to love her, I'm sure they warned him daily of what he would get himself into if he married her; but their report was not enough for Hosea. All he had was God's report that she was to be his wife and that was enough for him. Although this story was about Hosea and his obedience, Gomer shows us that no matter where we are, God does not leave or forsake us. He has already paid the price for us and delivered us out of the slavery of sin with the blood of his Son.

O *Tamar*

*But let up for yourselves treasures in heaven, where neither moth no rust doth corrupt, and where thieves do not break through or steal.* Matthew 6:2

# CHAPTER TWELVE

## Stolen Treasures

*For the thief cometh not but to kill, steal, and destroy...*
John 10:10

As we know things do not always start off good and sometimes life can take turns that we are simply not prepared for. If diamonds are a symbol of the 'good life', then it's not hard to believe that many people are in pursuit to attain them and that the journey of the diamond can be detoured by those who want it in their possession. Diamonds play a large part in the world of glitz and glamour and in the entertainment industry, where we see music videos with recording artists showcasing their diamond-laced watches, rings, medallions, and bracelets. Some recording artists even wear them in their teeth.

Diamonds are not only a hot commodity for women, but for thieves have also sought to possess the gem. Diamond smuggling movies have always shown these professional thieves stealing a handful of precious stones, somehow losing most of the gems in the course of the film, but managing to get away with at least one stone worth millions, tucked away in a pocket. Leakage is a common problem in the diamond plants and one uncut rough has a value of seven billion dollars a year! In situations portrayed on the big screen many people lose their lives over the greed for the diamond; these are even called Blood Diamonds. The diamond smugglers are majority of the time workers within the plant, and many times in earlier years it was the miners themselves. Securities in these plants have seen many methods used to smuggle diamonds. Thieves will hide diamonds behind sweatbands, inserted into razor cuts in tires, pressed under fingernails, and also wedged in between the grooves in the soles of boots. These diamonds are passed from thief to thief, all who play a part in misguiding the stone. How many times have we wandered through life feeling misguided and as if our very essence has been taken from us?

Unfortunately many of God's precious jewels are not always able to be kept free from harm's way. So many precious gems are suffering the negative effects of molestation, abuse, rape, sodomy, drug use and more. These are the layers and layers of stuff that have to be cut away and ground off by processing. Many of us harbor painful secrets from our childhood past and are carrying them over into our adulthood. God has need for you, but he can't use you if you are covered in the shame of your past. We all have something that we have been through, making our test our testimony and our mess our message.

Tamar was the daughter of King David. She had royalty running through both bloodlines, as her maternal grandfather was also a king. Her half-brother Amnon lusted after her and I'm sure his sexual advances and innuendos carried on for quite some time. She'd walk past him and hear his remarks and feel his lustful eyes upon her and it wasn't long before he would ask her for sex and she would deny him and become a victim of such an evil act as rape. Amnon was Tamar's stepbrother and was supposed to protect her, but his lust for her was far greater than Tamar could have imagined. Her security system had failed her; she was smuggled out of her innocence into a place that could potentially destroy her forever.

Amnon had broken her. He wounded her in her most intimate place – her heart. Its one thing to be broken by God, but it's another thing to be broken by someone else's violation. What she treasured most was taken away from her. No daughter of the King should ever be exploited, beaten, used or abused. She should be treated as regal, because that is the core and the essence of not only what she is, but who she is. Have you ever been broken? Have you ever been in that place where you've felt like you've lost everything and you have no more fight in you? How will you come up from that low place?

*Woman of Brilliance*, do you know that you are the daughter of the Most High God? Your bloodline is that of The King of Kings, Lord of Lord's. You are royalty! As long as you stay connected to the True Vine, you are covered by the blood. The enemy of your existence does not want you to know that you have purpose and destiny. He does not want you to know that your story doesn't end with what happened to you. He doesn't know that in the end he will be defeated.

What happened to you is not your testimony, but how the Lord redeemed you in the midst of it all is. Maybe you have actually gone through rape or molestation. Perhaps you are still dealing with the shame and embarrassment as you continue to carry it. Many of us have been misused, some abused, and misguided by those that we trust and love. Betrayal is the most hurting pain that one could endure. It hurts to know that someone you love could do anything to cause you any pain and especially on purpose. Think about Jesus. I am sure that it pained him to know that Judas was in his camp.

As humans our natural reaction to betrayal is to put up a wall to shield ourselves from receiving any more pain from that person. We build those walls on anger, bitterness and unforgiveness. It is hard to trust them the same, and it is just as hard to see past the act of betrayal, making it harder to forgive. And once the seed of unforgiveness plants itself in the soil of our heart, it produces a stony covering.

That old heart may still be hurting from the act of betrayal, but God is capable and willing to renew your spirit and take out that stony heart. Do you realize that a heart of stone is unable to feel anything? It has no compassion and it has no love. It is dead and hard as a rock. Have you ever stood at the water's edge and thrown a rock or a pebble? What happens to that rock when it hits the water? It sinks. And so does a stony heart. You will sink and drown in the sea of unforgiveness if you do not release those things you have been holding on to. If you don't let go, God can't grab your hand and hold you up. He can't work in a heart of stone. He needs to live in a fleshy heart, pumping His blood. As long as you hold someone in your prison of unforgiveness, they can never move on and neither can you. They will remain in a prison cell that you built and you are the Warden holding the key. Do you want to put in all those hours keeping watch over a prisoner of your unforgiveness? Release it today. Know that God has a plan for you. Yes, it is a shame that many gemstones like you have been hurt, betrayed, abused and used. Oftentimes the pain and the reality of the acts committed against us are never addressed, and resentment sets in. Some people have found solace and comfort in counseling, psychiatric therapy and even medication. The fact of the matter is that nothing can free you from the snares of the enemy – but the Almighty God. Whether the abuse is physical, mental, or verbal – let it go, move on, get going! Put everything at his feet, look up, and live! Intimacy with God will bring about change. Let God renew your mind and your spirit and give you a receptive heart of flesh that feels, loves, and most of all forgives.

## UNSET STONES

Maybe you are like Tamar; not raped physically against your will, but spiritually and emotionally raped by that brother that you thought loved you, the one that told you how much he cared for and loved you. He even promised that you would spend life together, but slowly the real person was revealed. Perhaps he left you for another woman and treats you like you never meant anything to him. Maybe you are still recovering from a divorce. Your divorce was not the end of you, being molested, raped, or physically abused doesn't even tell the end of your story! Yes it hurt you, bruised you – it may even have broken you down, but it doesn't mean that it is the end of you. It is those very things, those hidden things that God wants to deal with. Those secret hurts and things that haunt you and seem to torment your soul. Those things that speak volumes to you, but you don't want anyone else to hear. Your war is with the enemy, who comes not but to kill, steal and destroy (John 10:10). Distractions from the enemy come to steal time and take your focus off of God and rob you of your purpose in life.

CHAPTER THIRTEEN

# A Rough Recovery

*You therefore endure hardness, as a good soldier of Jesus Christ.*
2 Timothy 2:3

The Bible tells us that after the rape, Tamar was hated by Amnon. Her brother, Absalom even told her to forget about the incident and she lived as a desolate woman, forsaking her royal robe and settling for ashes (2 Samuel 3:18-20). Her brother Absalom would get revenge on Amnon, eventually killing him two years later out of hatred for what he did to Tamar. However, it is unclear if Tamar ever survived the rape emotionally, but it is clear that she did not take her shame to God.

Tamar pleaded with her half-brother and asked a profound question as she struggled to free herself from the grip of his hands. She asked him, "Where could I go in my shame?" *Woman of Brilliance*, if you've ever experienced shame in your life, where do you go with it? The answer to that question is to go to God with it. Take the shame for everything that you've been through and go to your heavenly Father with it. God has a great bartering system when dealing with our shame. If we freely admit to our shame and bring it to God, He will give us double for it (Isaiah 61:7-8). Whatever we have lost in the process of receiving shame, God will recompense us with twice as much. Get your joy back, get your peace back, get your smile back, and get it back double! *Woman of Brilliance*, you've been through some things, you've lost some things and some people along the way. No one really knows what you've been through, but God. Don't forfeit your royal garments like Tamar because of your pressure. God has ordered your steps *Woman of Brilliance*! During those times when you may have let your guards down and found yourself picking up the pieces of your broken heart – God has even worked the details out in that.

As some diamonds continue to slip through the security, today's mining industry has gotten a little harder for the miners to smuggle diamonds, as they rarely come into direct contact with a rough. Plants now have heavy machinery that scoops out the ore and sends it back into the plant for processing. Sometimes we have to avoid direct contact with those people, places, or things that could breach our spiritual security system. Sometimes we have to go back into the presence of the Father, to not only be hidden, but for more processing. In fact, it's a continual process before the Master Gemologist. While you are in your continual processing, put everything at His feet, look up, and live! Intimacy with God will bring about change. Let God renew your mind, heal your broken heart and change your story for His glory. Though the recovery is rough, it will be worth it.

## JEWELS IN HIS CROWN

*And the Lord their God shall save them in that day as the flock of his people: for they shall be as the stones of a crown, lifted up as an ensign upon his land* (Zechariah 9:16).

Before his expulsion from heaven, Lucifer was the most beautiful creation known. He was created as a worshipper and his body was made up of every instrument and it was covered in precious jewels. *Thou hast been in the Garden of God; every precious stone was thy covering, the sardius, topaz, and the diamond (*Ezekial 28:13). When he became full of pride, he lost his position and his place of worship. He was bound, but his instruments of worship were not, they are still worshipping God with the angels in Heaven. In fact, God has given some great musicians in the Body of

Christ those beautiful songs of praise and worship and those precious jewels God has placed them in the crown of Jesus.

*"For God, who commanded the light to shine out of darkness, hath shined in our hearts, to give the light of the knowledge of the glory of God in the face of Jesus Christ. But we have a treasure in earthen vessels, that the excellency of the power may be of God, and not of us."* 2 Corinthians 4: 6-7

Your brilliancy *is* the excellency of the power of God. It is time for your light to shine out of darkness. Find your praise *Woman of Brilliance*. It is your praise that will promote you out of that cold, dark pit and into your new faceted lifestyle of brilliance. Turn your pressure into praise! Praise will elevate you out of your rough place and bring you into a place of brilliance, where you can let your fiery light shine as an ensign in His crown. Everything that you have gone through and will go through in Jesus' name will be a testimony of His grace and mercy. God is a redeemer and a great recovery is about to take place in your life!

# CHAPTER FOURTEEN

## Protect Your Jewels

*Do not give what is holy to dogs, and do not throw your pearls*
*before swine, or they will trample them under their feet.*
2 Timothy 2:3

The diamond is the only thing that will outlast anything that you will ever own. Items of such value are not only treasured, but protected. You can't walk into any store and find your diamonds lying around anywhere. They are normally found in exquisite jewel cases under lock and key. You should always esteem yourself in the same manner, *Woman of Brilliance*. Most importantly, you should always be handled with care. Taking care of yourself is your first priority. There's nothing wrong with getting your hair and nails done or splurging on a nice outfit every now and again to make sure you always look your best. It is important for you to make sure that you continue to endure. Regular maintenance is necessary, so you must surrender yourself to time with the Master Gemologist, fasting, prayer, and never forsaking the fellowshipping with other gemstones like you! You must continue to be cleaned, greased with oil, polished, and shined!

Your setting is also important to the meaning of a diamond. The diamond dresser will make sure the stone is set in the best setting for it, one that will demand attention. We know diamond rings are more favored than a diamond pendant. Because your setting is your presentation to the world, likewise, make sure that whatever setting you are in, that you can be identified as a *Woman of Brilliance*. Don't carry yourself around like an unkempt stone, smudged, scratched, or wounded by being sold, pawned, mishandled and used. You should not be easily negotiated, but always representing something exquisite, something of value. Know your worth. Your price should always be above rubies – that of a rare diamond. You cannot be compared to anything.

You may be in your Eve stages, just uncovering the purpose of your existence; or like Esther after experiencing life's cuts, surviving the process of being made over and transformed. You may even be like Hanna, dealing with low self-esteem and the scars of a life under pressure. Perhaps you're already on course, following Jesus like Joanna; or like Gomer persuaded by something other than authentic love. Even if you are like Tamar, grieving from being abused and misused – you pressure still has purpose. It doesn't matter what tried to break you. God used it to make you. You will make it through the cutting, the grinding away of those rough edges only for God to bring out who you really are – not who people thought they knew.

You are a major investment to your Creator and he won't give up on you even when you think there's not another level he can take you to, He treasures you! God has placed so much on the inside of you and each step of your process is significant and strategic in the revelation of you! You will make it to your place of brilliance in the fullness of time; it will be revealed who you really are, who you were created to be – a uniquely designed, brilliant masterpiece.

Reference Bibliography:

Diamond Council of America: The Diamonds Professionals, 2005. *The Diamond Course*

*My Beloved Diamond,*

*It seems like it was just yesterday when I discovered you. I knew that you were the one. I handpicked you in the darkness because I saw something within you.*

**Something bright, something precious, something rare, something real….**

*Your inner beauty captivated me. After I brushed the ashes away; I saw that you had no shape to compliment your beauty within. Some parts of you were scarred and bruised, and it hurt me to know that you had been broken by the pressures and the pains of this life, but as I looked upon you I saw you in a whole new light.*

**I saw your sparkle, your flair, your beauty, your brilliance…**

*But, when I uncovered you and examined you, I realized that I would have to cut away the scars and abrasions in order to bring out the best in you. You have been through the worse, but now it's time to shine. Wear your brilliance in its greatest capacity, and know that you were made for a purpose!*

Love,

*The Master Gemologist*
GOD

*Gemstone Notes:*

Write down your thoughts as you uncover your brilliance while reading each chapter.

_____

_____

_____

_____

_____

_____

_____

_____

_____

_____

_____

_____

_____

_____

_____

_____

_____

_____

_____

# HOW TO USE THIS BOOK

(1) Read it and pass it on

(2) Start a women's group

(3) Hand them out on church visits

(4) Make them available at local businesses

(5) Use them at women's retreats and events

(6) Discover your own way to use them or visit
www.diamondsintheroughbook.com for
additional suggestions and tips

**www.DiamondsintheRoughbook.com**

www.ingramcontent.com/pod-product-compliance
Lightning Source LLC
LaVergne TN
LVHW051811080426
835513LV00017B/1902